MENTORIN
FOR SUCC

BULLET GUIDE

Hodder Education, 338 Euston Road, London NW1 3BH

Hodder Education is an Hachette UK company

First published in UK 2011 by Hodder Education

This edition published 2011

www.hoddereducation.co.uk

Typeset by Stephen Rowling/Springworks

Printed in Spain

MENTORING FOR SUCCESS

BULLET GUIDE

Steve Bavister and Amanda Vickers

About the authors

Amanda Vickers and Steve Bavister are directors of Speak First, a fast-growing global training and coaching consultancy that specializes in communication skills – including personal impact, managing the media, presentation skills, influencing, coaching and mentoring skills. They are experts in business communication and deliver training and coaching around the world for a wide range of organizations.

Before joining Speak First Amanda worked for a global bank, both within the business and ultimately in a senior learning and development role, in which she successfully managed a team of 60 people. Steve worked at a senior level for an international media company, where he was responsible for a staff of 80.

Steve and Amanda have Honours degrees in Psychology and are Master Practitioners of Neuro Linguistic Programming (NLP), which gives them a rich understanding of what makes people tick.

Steve and Amanda have written a number of books including *Essential NLP*, *Confident Coaching*, *Presenting with Impact* and *Confidence and Personal Impact*.

Contents

Introduction

Speak to anyone who has had a truly great mentor and you'll quickly learn how much value there is to be gained from it. Talk to those who have mentored others and you'll hear a similar story. From time to time you may also hear a few horror stories about mentoring relationships that have gone badly wrong.

If you're new to mentoring, don't worry. This Bullet Guide gives you all the key information you need to achieve great results. Whether you're a mentor or a mentee, you'll have lots of valuable tips and techniques at your fingertips. You'll learn why it's so important to make the right match and know how to avoid common pitfalls that get in the way of achieving the success you want. You'll be able to get off to a good start and understand why the best relationships are founded on trust and open communication.

Being clear about goals and what the mentee wants from the relationship is vital to success. The next challenge is keeping up the momentum and getting maximum value out of the time you have together. Mentoring sounds simple on the surface. But, to be successful, you need not only to share your knowledge and expertise but also to be a good listener who asks questions that get the mentee thinking deeply. This takes great interpersonal skills and highly developed self-awareness.

Some mentoring relationships have bumps along the way – perhaps both mentor and mentee are busy and meetings are cancelled or moved, or the 'chemistry' isn't quite right. If you're prepared for this and know what to do, it's easier to turn things round and get the relationship back on track or find someone new. There are plenty of pitfalls for the unwary, and this book will help you avoid them. After all, the whole purpose of mentoring is for the mentee to improve, to develop and to learn new things. To achieve this both mentor and mentee need to create a climate that supports and encourages the mentee to grow.

When it comes to the end of the allotted time it's important to bring things to a proper close. It's a time for reflection. Mentees may one day become mentors themselves. And mentors – well – they may get the bug and sign up for more of the same!

1 Understanding mentoring

There's more to mentoring than many people think. There's also much **more to gain for mentors** as well as mentees than you may have considered. Read on to **reap the rich rewards** that can be yours by understanding mentoring and how it leads to **increased success** in a wide range of fields.

Better than a thousand days of diligent study is one day with a great teacher.

Japanese proverb

Summary

This chapter will help you to:

* understand what mentoring is and is not
* recognize the many benefits that can be gained from mentoring relationships
* appreciate the wide range of situations where mentoring takes place
* know the difference between formal and informal mentoring
* learn about the roles and responsibilities of mentors and mentees.

What is mentoring?

Many people are confused about the differences among mentoring and coaching and other types of learning. It helps to be clear about each one.

Mentoring typically involves experienced people passing on their wisdom and knowledge. Mentors give advice and guidance by drawing on their business and life experiences.

Coaching is often confused with mentoring, but coaching is a largely **non-directive, goal-oriented collaboration** that helps people move forward rapidly. Many coaches don't give advice or guidance. They support the other person to come up with his or her own solutions.

Counselling is also non-directive. The focus is on **helping people overcome problems**, often by looking back at what's happened in the past.

Training is about passing on **information, skills and knowledge**. Training can be directive but is often delivered in a non-directive style to facilitate learning.

Managing involves giving direction to a subordinate. Managers are rarely mentors to their direct reports.

Directive				**Non-directive**
Managing	Training	Mentoring	Coaching	Counselling

Mentoring includes a mixture of directive and non-directive approaches.

The benefits of mentoring – win, win, win

Mentor

* **Gain personal satisfaction** from watching the mentee develop.
* Learn about what's happening at the 'grass roots' level.
* Take the opportunity to reflect on your own skills and knowledge.
* Develop interpersonal and coaching skills.
* **Leave a legacy** of your learning.

Mentee

* Gain rapid insight and fast-track progress.
* Benefit from exposure to an experienced role model.
* Get career and development advice.
* Obtain feedback from someone who is **one step removed.**
* Talk through ideas in a **safe environment.**
* Expand network of contacts.

The organization

* Develop and retain high-quality people.
* Improve communication and break down silos.
* Improve efficiency and productivity.
* Enhance transmission of **company values** and **cultures**.

CASE STUDY

Jermaine, like many mentors, has an **altruistic motive**. When he isn't bringing in business for his company in his role as an account manager or spending time with his family, he acts as a mentor to help young boys get a better life. He gets **great satisfaction** from seeing those boys find worthwhile employment.

Mentoring in organizations

Many organizations that **value people development** have formal or informal mentoring schemes.

1 Large corporations often set up formal schemes to help their people make faster progress and **expand their understanding of the business**.

2 In many professions, such as teaching, there are mentoring schemes so that those **new to the profession** can 'acclimatize' as quickly as possible.

3 Entrepreneurs and business owners often seek out mentors so that they **avoid pitfalls** and are able to **grow their businesses** rapidly.

4 Sports people, actors, singers and people in almost every field often speak of mentors who have **helped them achieve success**.

5 Mentors who work with **children and young adults** with disadvantaged backgrounds are sometimes called **befrienders**.

8

Formal vs informal mentoring relationships

Some mentoring relationships are formal – and set up as part of an organizational scheme – whereas others are informal. A more experienced person might take a newcomer **'under his wing'** (often formalized as a buddy system) or the novice might seek out a **'seasoned campaigner'** who can offer guidance.

Famous mentoring relationships

Mentee	Mentor
David Beckham	Bobby Charlton
Richard Branson	Sir Freddie Laker
Anthony Hopkins	Laurence Olivier
Christina Aguilera	Mariah Carey
Wolfgang Amadeus Mozart	Johann Christian Bach
Alexander the Great	Aristotle

The role and responsibilities of mentors

* **Share** personal experiences, knowledge, advice and contacts.
* Help mentees learn from **mistakes**.
* Support **aspirations** and **ambitions**.
* Offer a **sounding board** for ideas.

* **Challenge** assumptions.
* Offer **constructive feedback**.
* Provide a **non-judgemental space** for mentees.
* Respect **confidentiality** of information.

Where does 'mentor' come from?

In Greek mythology, when Odysseus went off to war he left his son, Telemachus, in the care of his old friend Mentor. Athena took the guise of Mentor to advise Telemachus to stand up to the men who were attempting to court his mother. Over time, the word *mentor* has come to mean someone who acts as a trusted advisor, coach, guide or teacher.

The role and responsibilities of mentees

Successful mentees are **ambitious**, interested in **new experiences and challenges** and **receptive to feedback**.

A mentee's responsibility is to:

1 **Ask questions** – your mentor probably asked the same questions at some stage in his or her career.
2 **Respect** the **confidentiality** and sensitivity of information that is shared with you.
3 **Initiate** mentoring sessions – don't wait for your mentor to contact you.
4 Take a **proactive approach** to planning your career and personal development.

When both mentor and mentee are clear about their roles and responsibilities it increases the chances of the relationship achieving success

2 Successful mentoring relationships

What makes one **mentoring relationship** magical and another fizzle out part-way through? Not every mentoring relationship is successful. You can **increase the odds** of getting the best out of mentoring by **eliminating problems** from the outset and making sure that you **make the right match**.

To have found a good mentor, is to have found a jewel.

Albert and Lema Nsah

Summary

This chapter will help you to:

* discover what makes a mentor effective
* identify the characteristics of great mentees
* understand how to make sure that there's a good match between mentor and mentee
* get support to grow your skills as a mentor
* find a mentor when there is no formal scheme available.

What makes a mentor effective?

The best mentors have certain personal traits that make them effective in helping their mentee to **achieve greater things**:

* They have to be **trustworthy** – without trust the mentoring relationship won't flourish.
* They know how to **motivate and inspire** their mentees.
* They have **humility** – they are never arrogant or out to satisfy their own ego.
* They are willing to **challenge and stretch** their mentees to be their best.
* They **accept and support** their mentees, regardless of what they do or say.

16

CASE STUDY

Nicky didn't get on well with her first mentor. She found him arrogant. He talked only about how great and successful he was, which she found irritating. He gave her the impression that he thought she was unlikely to achieve her aspiration to hold a senior position in the company. Nicky didn't ask him many questions for fear of being ridiculed.

Nicky's second mentor, Chris, was entirely different. Chris was willing to share all her experiences, including the mistakes she'd made. Nicky loved the way Chris believed in her ability to achieve her goals and challenged her on her thinking. She felt that she could ask Chris anything and not feel stupid.

What are the characteristics of successful mentees?

See how you stack up against our list of seven characteristics of successful mentees:

1 They are **keen to learn**.
2 They **respect** their mentor and the relationship.
3 They're **receptive** and open to different ideas.
4 They don't think they have **all the answers** already.
5 They're **open to feedback** and uncovering blind spots.
6 They **appreciate** what their mentor does for them.
7 They have the **courage** to try new things.

CASE STUDY

James was delighted when he discovered a mentoring scheme that gave him time with a senior manager he admired in the IT department, so that he could make rapid progress in his career. James was eager to learn and gained a lot from the feedback Amit gave him. Amit involved James in a project whereby he acquired new skills. Working with Amit also meant that James got up to speed quickly with how the IT function and the company as a whole operated. At the end of their relationship they continued to keep in touch from time to time. Two years later James was successful in getting the job he wanted when he applied for a role in the IT function.

You will get the best out of mentoring if the mentee approaches it with an open and appreciative mindset

Matching mentors to mentees

When you're part of a formal scheme the human resources function in your organization usually **matches mentors with mentees**. If you're a mentee who wants to identify your own mentor, you will also find that the following step-by-step process will ensure that there's a **good fit** with your mentor:

1 Define what you want from the mentoring relationship.
2 Think about your experience level, needs, aspirations and personality style.
3 Create a list of the key components you need in mentors, including area of expertise, interpersonal skills and commitment to mentoring.
4 Create a shortlist of mentors who match your requirements.
5 Agree a get-out clause in case the chemistry isn't right.

The matching process requires thought and consideration. Don't be afraid to walk away and find someone else if it's not working.

Why training is important and where to get help

While this book provides you with what you need to know to **get off to a great start** as a mentor or mentee, you may want to learn more.

If you're taking part in an in-house scheme, you may be **offered training**. It's hugely beneficial if this is for **matched pairs of mentors and mentees**. It allows you to **build a connection** with your new mentor/mentee.

You can find **support online** from the Business Mentoring Network, the International Mentoring Network Organization and the National Mentor Network.

Speak First Ltd (www.speak-first.com) is one of a number of companies that offers **training** to companies that run mentoring schemes.

Five ways to find a mentor when there's no formal scheme

1 Find the **brightest, most successful person** you know and ask them to be your mentor.
2 Look for someone who's already **accomplished what you want to achieve** and ask them.
3 Put yourself out there. **Network**. Mingle with people at events or conferences.
4 Join a professional association or organization and approach suitable individuals.
5 **Look right in front of your nose!** The perfect mentor may be a friend or someone at the gym.

How to make a start as a mentor

Want to become a mentor but there's no formal scheme available? Just tell your friends, family and colleagues what you have in mind, and before long you'll hear of someone who is interested in being your mentee.

3 The mentoring process

Don't know where to start when it comes to mentoring? Don't worry! Like many things in life, **mentoring goes through a number of phases** – a predictable sequence. Once you know the process, and what's expected at each stage, you'll feel more comfortable and confident.

> ## It is one of the most beautiful compensations of this life that no man can sincerely try to help another without helping himself.
>
> Ralph Waldo Emerson

Summary

This chapter will help you to:

* understand the mentoring process
* schedule meetings effectively
* know how best to keep in contact
* become aware of different options for mentoring
* appreciate the importance of reviewing progress
* bring the relationship to a satisfactory end.

Phases of the mentoring relationship

There is a typical 'arc' in a mentoring relationship. At the start there may be some uncertainty until you get to know each other. That's why **making a connection** – often called contracting – is essential. Over time, the mentee will **gain many valuable insights** and **take action** based on the mentor's advice. Progress is reviewed and ultimately the relationship comes to a close.

A simple way of recalling the key steps in the mentoring process is based around the acronym MENTOR:

Making a connection and contracting in the first meeting.
Exploration.
New insight and understanding.
Taking action.
Opening up opportunities, ongoing evaluation/monitoring.
Reviewing and relationship closure.

The dos and don'ts of scheduling meetings

Do

✔ Book meetings **in advance** where possible.
✔ Schedule meetings every four to six weeks.
✔ Allow **at least an hour** for each meeting and longer for the first session (two hours minimum).
✔ Give your mentor/mentee **adequate notice** if you need to reschedule, and re-book straight away.

Don't

✔ Leave it to the last minute to book a meeting.
✔ Lose momentum by leaving **long gaps** between meetings.
✔ Try to squeeze in a mentoring session where another meeting in your schedule may over-run and compromise it.
✔ Fail to show up for a meeting, forget to **let your mentor know** if you need to postpone or omit to re-book.

Keeping in contact

Three things for mentors to consider:

1 **Be flexible rather than fixed** – if the mentee needs timely help, be there for him or her.
2 **Have an 'open door'** – be available, but manage expectations.
3 **Agree boundaries** – do you want to be available 24/7 or only weekdays?

Three things for mentees to bear in mind:

1 **Don't hold back** – if an urgent problem arises, contact your mentor.
2 **Respect your mentor's time** – be patient.
3 **Stay within boundaries** – contact your mentor only at agreed times.

Basic human contact – the meeting of eyes, the exchanging of words – is to the psyche what oxygen is to the brain.

Martha Beck

CASE STUDY: TAKING ACTION BETWEEN MEETINGS

Katalina (the mentee) wanted to expand her network of contacts in the finance department because she was keen to get a better understanding of the work people did there. John (her mentor) recommended that she went to the finance department coffee point and got to know some people through informal networking, as he had found that strategy useful in the past.

At the next meeting Katalina reported back on three auditors she'd met and what she had learnt about their roles.

She also said she wanted to learn more about finance strategy, so John offered to introduce her to the department head over lunch.

Mentoring options

Telephone

Most mentoring takes place face to face, but **telephone can work surprising well**. It is easier to work around busy schedules when the mentor and mentee are in different places – possibly even different countries.

On the telephone you have to rely on what people say and the way they say it to know whether what you're doing is effective.

Online

E-mentoring is used in schools and universities because it provides students with access to experts, specialists and corporate mentors who can review their work online.

Other mentoring options

Mentoring can be **more than sharing knowledge, experience, wisdom and insight** – it can be practical as well. Here are four ways of doing more than just talking:

1 The mentor and mentee **attend a meeting or conference** together.
2 The mentee **assists with a project**, assignment or piece of work.
3 The mentee **shadows the mentor**, and sees him or her in action.
4 The mentor personally telephones a contact to **effect an introduction**.

Five secrets of reviewing progress

Regular reviews are essential in a longer mentoring relationship:

1 Ask the mentee if he or she is **getting what they want** from the relationship.
2 Find out from each other what would make the relationship even more effective.
3 Be willing to **make changes** and try out new ideas.
4 Explore **what stops you** from achieving what you want.
5 Have a mindset that is focused on **continuous improvement**.

Mentoring is a brain to pick, an ear to listen, and a push in the right direction.

John C. Crosby

Bringing the relationship to a close

At the end of whatever number of sessions or time duration you've agreed, you should reserve your last meeting to bring the relationship to a satisfactory close. This is an opportunity to **look back** and **celebrate success**.

It's also important to **look forward** and agree how the mentee will proceed independently. Of course, you **may decide to continue** the relationship after the initial period is up. If you do, it's still useful to **summarize your progress** at this point and re-contract for a defined period.

4 The first session

The **first meeting** in the mentoring relationship is an **important one**. If you get this right you're on the road to success. Get it wrong and the whole thing can fizzle out. It's the time when you lay the **foundation stones** for a **fruitful relationship** based on trust and open communication. It's also the time when you **agree on the goals** the mentee wants to achieve.

Without rapport nothing is possible. With rapport anything is possible.

Milton H. Erickson

Summary

This chapter will help you to:

* create the right environment
* agree how you will work together
* recognise why confidentiality is crucial
* connect with each other easily and quickly
* understand the importance of building trust
* establish SMART goals
* prepare for success.

Creating the right environment

Creating the right environment for mentoring meetings is essential for success.

Do

✔ Hold your meeting in a place where mentor and mentee will **feel relaxed**.
✔ Consider a venue **away from the workplace** if this is appropriate.
✔ Opt for **comfortable chairs** where possible.
✔ Place the **seats at an angle** that encourages open discussion.

Don't

✘ Select a place where you can be overheard.
✘ Allow interruptions, take calls or check emails during the meeting.
✘ Create a barrier by sitting opposite each other across a table.
✘ Use a room that's too hot or too cold to be comfortable.

Agreeing how you will work together

It's important to **create a contract** for how you will work together going forward. This includes:

* agreeing **who schedules meetings** – the mentee usually owns this
* agreeing what happens if either person **needs to reschedule**
* the importance of keeping what is discussed confidential
* **how you'll work together** – what the expectations are on both sides
* how and when you will **end the relationship**.

In the first meeting you will also discuss:

* the mentee's objectives for the mentoring relationship
* any **actions** the mentee agrees to take before the following meeting
* the **date of the next meeting** – and possibly the whole series of them.

Keeping things confidential

It is crucial for mentors and mentees to agree up front that **conversations will be confidential**. This forms a **foundation of trust**. Skip this part and you'll end up with problems down the line.

There are **rare exceptions,** which you can flag up as part of your **agreement**. If you become aware of someone breaking company rules, for instance, or doing something illegal, you have a duty to let others know.

If either mentor or mentee wants to share the content of their conversations with anyone else, it must be **agreed beforehand**.

Keeping things confidential is the first building block for a great relationship

Connecting with each other

When you have **rapport** you are **relaxed** in each other's company. To truly connect with others you need to be present and take a **genuine interest** in them and what they want to achieve.

Establish a connection with your mentor or mentee as soon as possible, and **deepen the connection** as the relationship progresses.

Six ways to deepen the connection
1 *Be present* – not distracted by other things.
2 *Be interested* – even when it's a challenge.
3 *Be fully engaged* – truly listen.
4 *Match body language* – move as they do.
5 *Match voice* – volume, pace and pitch.
6 *Match language* – use their words.

Establishing trust

Trust is **fundamental** to effective mentoring. If a mentee is fearful of what their mentor might think of them or wonders if what they say will be used against them they won't get the same **value** from the relationship.

To establish trust mentors need to build **rapport** and create a **safe environment** that supports and encourages **open communication**. The mentee then feels comfortable enough to be open with their mentor.

Mentees trust their mentors if they perceive them to be **trustworthy**. This means that the mentor's behaviour matches his or her values. They have **integrity** – they do what they say they will do.

Establishing goals

If you don't know where you're going how can you expect to get there?

Basil S. Walsh

Sometimes, but not always, the mentee will want to **set goals** for their mentoring, so they have a **clear focus** and a **sense of achievement** at the end. A popular and effective model is **SMART**.

Specific	Goals should be specific rather than vague or woolly
Measurable	You should be able to clearly tell when they are achieved
Achievable	They need to be within your control and a stretch – but still attainable
Relevant	They should be consistent with other goals and fit with your sense of self
Time-bound	There needs to be a clearly defined deadline for achieving your goal

Bullet Guide: Mentoring for Success

Preparing for success

Devote the first part of the meeting to **getting to know each other** better. Some people find that it helps to tell the other person about other aspects of their life, such as family, hobbies or interests.

You could then move on to talk about other learning experiences/relationships you've had. Describe what you find works well for you and what doesn't. Sharing something about what **motivates** you can be helpful too.

5 Getting the best out of subsequent meetings

It's not enough to get off to a good start with mentoring. The key to success lies in **keeping up the momentum** and making the most of the time you have together. Experienced mentors recognize the value of following up effectively and sharing not only **knowledge** but also **contacts** from within their network.

> **We keep moving forward, opening new doors and doing new things, because we're curious – and curiosity keeps leading us down new paths.**
>
> Walt Disney

Summary

This chapter will help you to:

* follow up effectively on actions
* make the most of your time in meetings
* guide and support your mentee
* dig down to a deeper level
* understand your mentee's world
* share your wisdom effectively
* use your network to support your mentee.

Checking in

A common, and useful, way of making sure that **each meeting connects with the previous one** and builds on it is for the mentor to start by 'checking in' with the mentee. A lot can happen between sessions, and what seemed to be a pressing issue last time can sometimes be a distant memory now.

Don't assume that things are as they were, and the mentee will want to talk about the same things this time as last time. People often move on. A month can be a long time in business. Simple but effective checking in questions are:

* What has happened since we last spoke?
* How have things been?
* Could you give me an update?

Reviewing progress

Mentees often commit to completing certain tasks between sessions –
and it's important to follow up.

Do

✔ *Follow up* on commitments
  they made.
✔ Ask '*How did you do* with
  your "homework".'
✔ Find out what they've done
  that *moves them* towards
  their goals.
✔ Check that they feel real
  progress is being made.

Don't

✘ Forget what they said they
  would do.
✘ Nag if they haven't done their
  'homework'.
✘ Lose focus on the goals they are
  working towards.
✘ Worry if things are not always
  moving forwards quickly.

How would you like to spend the time?

Unless there's a good reason, it should be the mentee who 'drives' the session, setting the agenda for what he or she would like to discuss. So a good way to open each discussion is for the mentor to ask 'How would you like to spend the time?'

Guiding your mentee

The **primary** role of the mentor is to **offer guidance**. Here are some **dos and don'ts**:

Do

✔ Give advice based on your experience.
✔ Understand the issue thoroughly by asking lots of questions.
✔ Be balanced in your guidance.

Don't

✘ **Insist that** the mentee **does** what you advise.
✘ Offer an opinion when you **don't really understand** the issue.
✘ State your opinion as if it's the only option.

Going deeper

It's all too easy for mentoring to become a **cosy chat** – which can be pleasant and useful – but you should aim for it to be more than that. The secret lies in the mentor probing to understand the mentee's world at a deeper level.

Asking questions that go deeper can be like peeling back layers of an onion. The questions require the mentee to 'go inside' for the answer. Exploring your mentee's beliefs can open up new ways of thinking.

> ## You can have anything you want if you will give up the belief that you can't have it.
>
> Dr Robert Anthony

The spider diagram opposite shows some of the areas that should be explored, and some of the questions that could be asked.

Hopes and fears
What would they like to achieve?
What would make them most happy?
Where would they like to be in 5 years?
What are they most afraid of?
What keeps them awake at night?
What do they avoid?

Beliefs
What are the rules they live by?
What must they do?
What should they do?
What do they believe about others?

Experience
What have they done already?
What did they like/dislike?

Understanding the mentee's world

Values
What's important to them?
What do they care about most?

Strengths and weaknesses
What are their strengths?
What are their weaknesses?

Identity
How do they see themselves?
Is that how they would like to be?
What do they like/dislike?
What is their ideal self?

Sharing wisdom and experience

One of the ways in which the mentor **offers guidance** is by **sharing** his or her **experience**. This can be done by:

* sharing 'war stories' relating to the mentee's issue
* discussing how a different problem was handled and the outcome
* recounting experiences appropriate to the situation.

Introducing mentees to people in the mentor's network

1 If your mentee wants a **better understanding** of your organization, introduce him or her to people from different parts of it.
2 There are two ways of moving things forward:
   a Ask your mentee to call or email your contact, **mentioning your name.**
   b Send an email to both your mentee and your contact, suggesting that they **link up.**
3 Ask your mentee to **accompany you** to events and introduce him or her to people in your network face to face.

Ask yourself
*Whom would it have been useful for you to have known **early in your career**? Those are the people you need to introduce to your mentee.*

6 Skills of successful mentors – and mentees

Anyone can share their knowledge and expertise. That alone isn't enough to make you a successful mentor. You need to be a **good listener** and **ask questions** to make sure that the information you give is what your mentee really needs. Great mentors have **great interpersonal skills**. They have highly developed **self-awareness**, **experience in coaching** others and the **ability to build and maintain rapport** with people. Mentees can benefit from these skills too.

> **The most important single ingredient in the formula of success is knowing how to get along with people.**
>
> Theodore Roosevelt

Summary

This chapter will help you to:

* understand how to give advice in an effective way
* get the balance right between talking and listening
* harness the power of asking great questions
* listen actively at a deeper level
* give constructive and supportive feedback
* nurture creativity and innovation in your mentee
* adapt your behavioural style to match your mentee's.

Two ears, one mouth

Mentors need to **strike a balance** between talking and listening to the mentee. As the saying goes, 'You have two ears and one mouth and should use them in that proportion'. Most of us aren't as good at listening as we could be. It takes effort. You need to **stop thinking about what you want to say next** and truly listen to the other person.

I like to listen, I have learned a great deal from listening carefully. Most people never listen.

Ernest Hemingway

Listening at three levels

There are three levels of listening.

1 We just hear what people say at a superficial level.
2 We really hear and think about what's been said.
3 We listen with our eyes as well as our ears and pick up emotions.

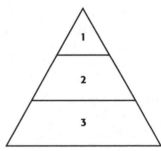

You can go deeper still by **listening for what's not being said**. What is your mentee avoiding or ignoring at a conscious or unconscious level? By drawing attention to these things you open the door to **new perspectives and insights** into the situation.

Mentees need to be tuned in to pick up **subtle nuances** in the way their mentor expresses things too, so that they can get a richer understanding of what is being said.

The power of questioning

Effective mentors often take a **coaching approach**. This means **asking questions** that help the mentee **develop understanding** for themselves, rather than being 'spoon fed' solutions by the mentor.

Five top tips for asking powerful, effective questions:

1 **Ask open questions** that start with who, what, when, where and how.
2 **Minimize 'why' questions:** they tend to produce a justification or a defensive answer.
3 **Useful words** to open discussion include 'Tell me …', 'Say more …' or 'Describe …'
4 Powerful questions probe – and **go deeper** into the issue.
5 Avoid **'leading'** questions that **imply a point of view** or specific answer.

66

The funnel technique

Start with broad questions, then narrow the focus.

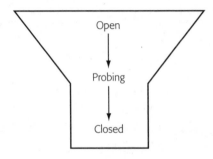

Advice about giving advice

* Avoid the temptation to enjoy an **ego trip** and talk about all your successes.
* Ask questions to check that the advice you're giving is targeted to what the mentee needs.
* Focus on how your experience can best benefit the mentee's situation.
* Give the mentee a chance to ask questions – **don't talk at length**.
* Summarize your key points, so that it's clear what you're saying.

TOP TIP FOR MENTEES
If your mentor's advice doesn't seem to fit your situation, **accept it in the spirit in which it's offered** and provide him or her with more information so that he or she can better understand your situation.

Ten tips for giving constructive feedback

Giving constructive feedback is an **essential skill** in mentoring. You need to make sure that it is …

1 **Specific** – not general or abstract, and includes examples.
2 **Objective** – not based on opinion but on firm evidence.
3 **Honest** – not 'sugar coated', and expressed freely and clearly.
4 **Simple** – too much detail is overwhelming and undermining.
5 **Sensitive** – think about what it would be like to receive it.
6 **Positive** – let mentees know what specifically they did well.
7 **Practical** – relates to something mentees can do something about.
8 **Supportive** – it arises from wanting to make things better.
9 **About the behaviour** – it's about the task or action taken, not the person.
10 **Accepting** – non-judgemental, seeing the real person in front of you.

Nurture creativity and innovation

Enthusiasm is excitement with inspiration, motivation and a pinch of creativity.

Bo Bennett

One benefit mentees get from having a mentor is that they have someone to **bounce ideas off**.

Meetings can provide a perfect environment for coming up with **creative solutions to problems** and innovative approaches to situations the mentee faces. If the mentee wants to find a new job, for instance, the mentor can help him or her come up with a **range of possibilities**.

Match your mentee's style

People are different. Some are task oriented, and for others people come before tasks. Some are **quiet** and **introvert** and others are **loud** and **extrovert**. Some people like to think before they act or say something. Others work out what they think by talking.

There's **no right or wrong** – just difference. To be effective you need to **adapt your style** to the other person's.

CASE STUDY

Henry's mentor, Eva, is gregarious, people oriented and talks quickly. Henry is analytical, task oriented and speaks slowly. Eva and Henry both *adapt their approach* when they meet. Eva attempts to slow down and add detail to her explanations. Henry takes time for a coffee and a social chat before they get down to business.

7 Bumps along the way

Some mentoring relationships run smoothly, but many have some bumps along the way. This is often because either or both parties are busy, and logistical problems arise. Sometimes it's because of lack of commitment on the part of the mentor or mentee. Occasionally it's because the 'chemistry' isn't quite right. Expect some bumps along the way, and you'll be prepared for them when you hit them.

> **It is not because things are difficult that we do not dare, it is because we do not dare that things are difficult.**
>
> Seneca

Summary

This chapter will help you to:

* anticipate and manage any 'bumps'
* know how to deal with contact issues
* manage any problems with chemistry
* cope if the mentee runs out of issues
* deal with frustration arising for various reasons.

Lack of or infrequent contact

Most mentors and mentees start out with the best of intentions, but sometimes business or life gets in the way. Scheduled meetings get postponed. Someone cancels at the last moment. A couple of months pass with no meeting …

Do

✔ At least speak on the phone – you can surely find 30 minutes to connect and catch up.

✔ Ring-fence mentoring discussions – only cancel them if there really is no choice.

✔ Be creative in finding ways of keeping in touch.

Don't

✘ Let a long period pass without at least trying to find a mutually convenient time to speak with each other.

✘ Consider mentoring discussions to be optional and easily cancelled.

✘ Give up too easily and say that it can't be done.

One party distracted and not fully present

Mentors and mentees need to be **fully present** – and **fully committed** – if the session is to be successful and the relationship is to work. It's all too easy to let your mind wander.

Worse still, some mentors have been known to break off in the middle of a session to attend to an urgent business matter. You may get away with this once, but any more than that and the mentee will feel that you think that he or she is not important. Actions speak louder than words!

You may think that you get away with it but you won't. They will notice

When the chemistry isn't right

What if you don't hit it off with your mentor or mentee? Here are four things you can do …

1 **Try to make it work** Sometimes it takes a while for people to get on to the same wavelength. Stick with it. Work at it.
2 **Figure out what's going on** What's the problem? Personality? Background? Attitude? See if you can pinpoint what the problem is.
3 **Put it on the table** Say to the other person, 'I'm not sure that this is working, we don't seem to be gelling.' Maybe he or she feels the same. Perhaps he or she has a solution.
4 **See if you can swap** No point in banging your head against a brick wall. If it isn't working, move on if you can, perhaps swapping to someone else.

Mentee runs out of 'issues'

CASE STUDY

The first two sessions Amit and his mentor, Sara, had together went really well. Amit raised a number of issues, and Sara was able to share her experience of similar situations and offer valuable advice.

During the third session, however, things seemed to go flat. Amit didn't have any pressing problems, and Sara struggled to come up with suggestions that seemed useful.

In situations like this it's useful to remember that the mentor's role is not only to give advice and share knowledge. Mentors can help to solve problems and deal with issues, and play a much wider role. So don't worry if you run out of problems and issues. Simply explore other areas.

Frustration at lack of progress

Sometimes mentees gain a lot from their mentoring very quickly. Other times it can feel as if there's a lack of progress – discussions plateau and 'stick' on the third or fourth session.

Tips for maintaining progress:

* Both mentor and mentee should **prepare for the session**, not just turn up.
* Mentees **need to be clear** about what they want and what they need.
* Mentors should **take time to reflect** on what they could usefully share.
* If 'stuckness' continues, look for **creative ways** of generating more energy.

Mentor lacks experience to help with the mentee's issue

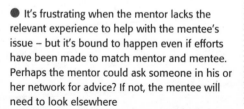

How can you motivate your team better? No idea! But I can help you improve your spreadsheet skills.

● It's frustrating when the mentor lacks the relevant experience to help with the mentee's issue – but it's bound to happen even if efforts have been made to match mentor and mentee. Perhaps the mentor could ask someone in his or her network for advice? If not, the mentee will need to look elsewhere

Mentee expects too much

When our expectations are high we often **end up disappointed** – and that can certainly happen in mentoring. If the mentee expects that mentoring will provide knowledge and insight that will **propel him or her to the top**, a reality check is likely to follow soon after.

Mentors should follow this process in order:

1 Clarify the mentee's expectations.
2 Manage those expectations.
3 Check in periodically with the mentee.
4 Re-manage the mentee's expectations.

82

The mentor moves on

People change jobs or leave organizations. What do you do if your **mentor moves on** and is unable to work with you again? Accept the situation with resignation and find yourself a new mentor.

8 Taking it to the next level

Imagine coming to the end of your mentoring relationship and the mentee is exactly the same as when you started. If you were the mentor how would you feel? What if you were the mentee? It's likely you'd both feel that it was a complete waste of time and effort. The whole purpose of mentoring is for the mentee to **improve**, to **grow** and to **learn new things**. To achieve this, both mentor and mentee need to create a climate that **supports and encourages** the mentee to stretch him- or herself.

... by stretching yourself beyond your perceived level of confidence you accelerate your development of competence.

Michael J. Gelb

Summary

This chapter will help you to:

* 'hold your mentee big'
* inspire your mentee to achieve more
* encourage a 'can do' attitude
* provide your mentee with support when needed
* raise your mentee's visibility and expand his or her horizons
* follow up when your mentee agrees to take action.

Hold them big

If you're the mentor, **focus** not just on the person in front of you but also on his or her **potential** – 'hold them big'. When you think in this way – that your mentees are 'up for something big' – they'll sense that you believe in them without your having to say it explicitly. What you hold to be true about people is evidenced in everything you do and say.

To get the most out of the mentoring relationship when you're the mentee, you need to **believe in yourself**. What else could you learn from your mentor? Let him or her know that you **appreciate the advice** and ask what else he or she thinks it would be good for you to learn or do next.

Be a role model who inspires others

CASE STUDY

Emma was a graduate entrant to the company. Although she was bright, she lacked confidence in her ability to make it in the business world. Her mentor, Althea, told her a story about when she was young and starting out and how nervous she had been back then. She went on to describe how she had made the transition to a place where she could enjoy speaking to large groups of 200 or more. 'If Althea can do it,' Emma thought, 'I can do it too!'

Six ways to foster a 'can do' attitude

1 Listen for **'can'ts'** in what the mentees say, and find ways of turning them into **'cans'**.
2 When mentees agree to do something, pin them down to a **deadline**.
3 Encourage mentees to **believe in their own ability** to do what they want to do.
4 Use 'make it happen' and 'why not do it now?' language to put **momentum** behind them.
5 Make what they want to achieve sound **exciting** rather than like a mountain to climb.
6 Be a **role model** they can emulate for getting things done.

90

Be a cheerleader!

When we set ourselves stretching goals or attempt something for the first time and **experience a setback**, it's easy to lose confidence. That's when mentors need to turn into cheerleaders – offering encouragement and support when it's most needed.

If, for example, your mentee needs to complete a project and is feeling unsure that he or she can pull it off, remind them of another situation in which they did something that required similar skills. If you genuinely **believe in their ability,** they will start to believe in themselves too.

A few simple words of support are often all it takes to get people **back on track**.

Raise your mentee's visibility

One of the great things about mentoring is that it often allows mentees to raise their visibility within their organization – and sometimes outside too.

What you help mentees to do

* Encourage them to consider how they want to be perceived by others.
* Ask them how other people see and experience them now.
* Get them to **identify the gap** between where they are and where they want to be.
* Help them to make the changes necessary to get there.
* Ask them to examine how they represent themselves on social networking sites.

What you – the mentor – can do

* Introduce them to people in your network.
* Where you feel able to, **recommend their work** to others.
* Invite your mentees to **join you at events** so that they get practical exposure to your world.
* Tell them how you raised your profile and how you continue to do so.

Mentors can help, but ultimately it's the mentee's responsibility to raise his or her own profile

Expanding mentees' horizons

One **valuable thing** a mentor can do for mentees is expand their 'horizons' – helping them think beyond what their focus was at the beginning of the relationship. From their more elevated vantage point of having **more experience** – and more often than not expertise and/or seniority – mentors can help their mentees become aware of possibilities and opportunities they perhaps would never have thought of on their own.

Do

✔ *Be open to new ideas (if you're a mentee) and offer them if you're a mentor.*

✔ *Offer suggestions for the other person to consider.*

Don't

✘ *Just follow the same path you've walked down a thousand times.*

✘ *Try to impose your ideas on your mentee.*

Following up

When mentees agree to do something between sessions:

1 **Make a note of the action** they said they will take.
2 **Check in with them** towards the start of the next session to find out how they are getting on with it.
3 If they've completed it, **congratulate them** on their achievement.
4 If they haven't, **probe** to find out what stopped them.
5 Help them to find a way around any obstacles.
6 Remember **you're not their mum** – it's not your place to 'tell them off'.

Mentees often set out with **full expectations** of fulfilling the commitment they make to themselves and then find that it doesn't happen. They have a deadline to meet. A colleague asks for help. Or they simply change their mind about it. It can help to **discuss this with your mentor** at your next session.

9 Common pitfalls

In any endeavour there are **potential pitfalls or traps** the unsuspecting person can fall into. Most of us **learn the hard way** from experience. That's the great value of having a mentor – you can steer clear of most of the pitfalls and accelerate your achievement of success. This chapter is packed full of **advice** on how to avoid or overcome the common problems mentors and mentees face.

> **Good things don't come easy.**
> **The road is lined with pitfalls.**
> Desi Arnaz

Summary

This chapter will help you to:

* avoid common problems mentors and mentees face
* know what to if your mentor or mentee talks too much
* avoid patronizing your mentee
* understand the difference between mentoring and management
* understand the importance of avoiding being indiscreet
* recognize the importance of honouring professional boundaries
* take action when your mentee has a hidden agenda
* know what to do if your mentor falls from favour.

Talking too much

Some people love talking. This can be a problem in mentoring – if the mentor or mentee **doesn't know when to stop**. It's easy to fill an hour with the mentor sharing every experience he or she has had on a topic, along with a few 'interesting' stories that are almost, but not quite, on the subject.

Equally, a mentee might pack the time full with **endless examples** of what he or she has done since the last session, leaving hardly any of the session for moving forward with his or her goal.

Focus on **sticking to the point** being discussed and make sure that you **use the time effectively**.

100

Being patronizing and/or dictatorial

It's all too easy for mentors to **assume their mentee knows little or nothing** – and hand down their pearls of wisdom in a patronizing way. But mentees often know more than you might think. So always check first, before launching into a long, pointless lecture.

Some mentors go further and insist that their mentees carry out recommendations to the letter. They may get upset, frustrated or even angry when mentees don't respond in the way they would like.

> **Look closely at those who patronize you.**
> **Half are unfeeling. Half are untaught.**
>
> Johann Wolfgang von Goethe

Straying from mentoring into management

Responsibilities of mentor	Responsibilities of mentee's line manager
To agree **goals** to focus on during the relationship	To set and agree goals and targets
To advise on performance issues if asked	To manage performance
To inspire and motivate	To create a motivating environment
To coach and develop	To coach and develop

When the mentor starts to act like a line manager and starts managing the mentee's performance, the mentee **misses out on the value of an independent relationship** and may also receive mixed messages.

When it comes to motivation and coaching, both mentor and line manager get involved.

Being indiscreet

Do

✔ Keep what is discussed between the two of you.
✔ Only talk to someone else about the content of your session *if you have the other person's permission* to do so.
✔ Tell someone if the other person does something illegal.

Don't

✘ *Blur the line* by telling someone else a 'snippet' of information.
✘ Discuss what you dislike or find amusing about the other person's behaviour with others.
✘ Conceal anything the mentor or mentee does that is against the law.

Overstepping the professional boundary

When mentors and mentees connect well it's all too easy for the relationship to **shift from formal to friendly**, and then – if they're not careful – to **familiar**. You may be thinking, 'What's the problem with that?' Imagine for a moment that your mentee asks you out on a date!

It could work the other way round. What if your mentor oversteps the professional boundary?

Familiar means different things to different people. What do you do?

1 **Reinforce the boundary** by making it clear what the limits are for you.
2 Decline invitations that blur the line between friendly and familiar.
3 If this doesn't work, and you still feel uncomfortable, **consider finding a new mentor or mentee.**

Deliver on promises

Do ...

- ✔ What you say you will do.
- ✔ Make enough time available for your mentee.
- ✔ Effect introductions in a timely way.
- ✔ Respond to emails and calls within 24 hours.
- ✔ Be a role model for honesty and integrity.

Don't ...

- ✘ Say one thing and then do something else.
- ✘ Arrive late or make the session feel rushed.
- ✘ Finally send an email introduction weeks later.
- ✘ Fail to reply or respond after two or three weeks.
- ✘ Tell fibs, exaggerate or bend the truth.

**Promise only what you can deliver.
Then deliver more than you promise.**
Unknown

Mentee has a hidden agenda

CASE STUDY

Jack suspected that his mentee, Ben, had a **hidden agenda**. Ben asked him if he could join him when he visited a private, members only golf function. He also requested many more introductions to people in Jack's professional network than Jack had experienced with mentees he had worked with in the past. He decided to have a talk with Ben to find out if his assumption was correct and **reinstate the boundaries** of the mentoring relationship.

Integrity is doing the right thing, even if nobody is watching.

Anonymous

Mentor falls from favour

Occasionally you may find that your mentor starts out as a **shining example** of all you aspire to and then **falls from favour**. People are human. They make mistakes. The tips below are invaluable if this happens to you:

* **Almost every successful person makes mistakes and learns from them**. Look for what you can learn so that you avoid doing the same thing.
* **Take the best from your mentor**. Disregard anything that doesn't fit with your values.
* **Be understanding and empathic**. People make the best choices they can with what's available to them at the time.
* **Know where to draw the line**. If your mentor has done something immoral or illegal end the relationship and look for someone else.

10 Bringing things to a successful close

They say that **all good things come to an end**, and that's true when it comes to mentoring. Running the last meeting as normal and then just saying goodbye can feel strange for both mentor and mentee. **Things need to be brought to a proper close**. Once you know how to wrap things up in the best possible way, you'll feel confident in your ability to bring things to a close successfully.

> **A mentor is someone who allows you to see the hope inside yourself.**
> Oprah Winfrey

Summary

This chapter will help you to:

* recognize the value of reflecting on the journey you have taken together
* prepare effectively for your final meeting
* build confidence by celebrating success
* leave the mentee in a good place
* consider what mentors learn during the relationship
* create a plan for the future and putting the learning into practice.

Reflecting on the journey

The final session is usually set aside for reflecting on the journey you've made together – and 'what next?'

It's useful for mentors and mentees to consider the **knowledge and insights** they've shared and gained.

112

Both might also consider how the mentee can maintain and build on what he or she has learnt.

Tips for mentors: preparing for success

The questions below will help stimulate your thinking on how to make this important meeting a success:

* Think back to the first meeting. What knowledge, skills or attributes did the mentee display? **How has this changed?**
* What **obstacles** did the mentee overcome?
* What **achievements** should the mentee be proud of?
* What **advice** can you give the mentee to help with his or her **ongoing development**?

Tips for mentees: getting the most out of the final meeting

* Reflect on how things were when you started. What **progress** has been made with your goals? What is still work in progress?
* What **challenges** did you face?
* What went well and why?
* What do you still want to work on? What **support** do you need to help you?

Celebrating success

All too often in life people **focus on their weaknesses** – what's not working or how they can improve. While this is useful, the power of **recognizing what we're good at**, what we've achieved and how much we've progressed cannot be overstated. In the drive to be better we don't make time to **build on our strengths** and **celebrate success**.

It's important to find time to **focus on achievements** that the mentee is proud of and strengths that he or she can **capitalize on** in the future.

CASE STUDY

Elie was looking forward to her final session with her mentor. She was **pleased with all the knowledge she had gained**. She was also delighted with how well her new team were responding after a wobbly start.

During the final meeting Sam placed most of the **emphasis on what Elie still needed to learn** and emphasized how much she still needed to adapt her approach to get the team motivated. While she valued the extra pointers **she left feeling a little deflated**.

Celebrate what you want to see more of.

Thomas J. Peters

Leaving the mentee in a good place

It's vital that mentors and mentees set aside time to wind things up properly before the end of the session. It's important for mentors to leave their mentee in a good place.

Tips for mentors: four steps for structuring the final session

1 Begin by explaining the purpose of the final meeting.
2 Check whether the mentee has any **outstanding areas** that haven't been covered.
3 Invite the mentee to share his or her experience of the mentoring period and **what he or she has gained from it**.
4 Add anything that the mentee has missed. **Celebrate successes** – even the small ones. Your aim should be to raise the mentee's awareness of their progress.

What has the mentor gained – and learnt?

It's not only mentees that gain from the relationship – mentors, as we've seen, often **benefit enormously**. So the final session allows the mentor also to reflect on what has gone well, and less well.

One of the best ways of doing this is to **get some feedback** from the mentee. What did the mentor do that was good and effective? What didn't work as well – or even got in the way? What could the mentor **do better in the future**, if he or she supports someone else?

Assuming that an **open, supportive** and **honest** relationship has developed, an 'exit' discussion of this kind provides the perfect opportunity for the mentor to get valuable suggestions for improving his or her mentoring in the future.

What next?

So that's it. **You've had the last session**. You're going your separate ways. You may never see each other again. Some people feel a **sense of loss** when a mentoring relationship comes to an end.

What next? Here are some ways to keep up the momentum:

Share your skills
Share your experiences with would-be mentors

Find another mentee
You'll have learnt a lot – don't let that experience go to waste

Mentor

Set up a scheme
If there's no formal scheme, start one

Maintain contact
You can still support your former mentee informally

Look for other ways of developing
How to fill the gap? Perhaps by shadowing, further training or reading to build on your skills and knowledge

Stay in touch
There's no reason you can't stay in touch – but on a more casual basis

Mentee

Find another mentor
There's nothing to stop you – so think about the qualities you want

Become a mentor yourself
Knowing the value of mentoring, you'll have a lot to give as you gain experience

In my end is my beginning.
T.S. Eliot